DIESELS AROUND LONDON
A Colour Portfolio
David Cross

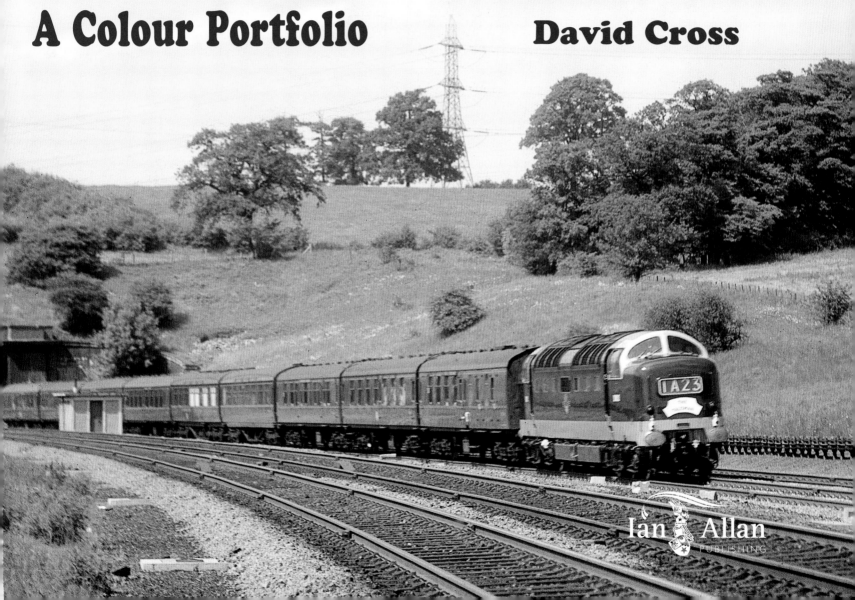

Ian Allan
PUBLISHING

Front cover: Seen at Subway Junction, brand-new 'Warship' No D826 *Jupiter* passes an inbound DMU as it leaves Paddington with the afternoon parcels for Plymouth on 10 September 1960. Introduced to traffic just 10 days earlier from Plymouth Laira, the locomotive would be withdrawn from the same depot in May 1973. *R. C. Riley*

Back cover: Spotters young and old look on as brand-new 'Deltic' No D9007 *Pinza*, named after the racehorse that won the 1953 Derby in the hands of legendary jockey Sir Gordon Richards, creeps into Platform 8 at King's Cross. Being driven from the 'wrong' end, the locomotive is backing down onto a train for Edinburgh Waverley. Having entered service at Finsbury Park in June 1961, it would see 20 years' top-link service on the East Coast main line before being withdrawn in December 1981 from York depot. *Derek Cross*

Previous page: The nine-coach up 'Talisman' from Edinburgh passes through Ganwick, just 11 miles from King's Cross, in late May 1961. The train is hauled by new 'Deltic' No D9003, as yet unnamed; note that, as delivered, the 'Deltics' had a large British Railways crest in the centre of the body where the name — in this case *Meld*, after the racehorse which won the fillies' 'Triple Crown' (the Oaks, St Leger and One Thousand Guineas) in 1955 — would later be affixed. Turned out by English Electric's Vulcan Foundry at Newton-le-Willows, Lancashire, in March 1961, this locomotive was to spend almost its entire life allocated to Finsbury Park depot, from where it would be withdrawn (as No 55 003) in December 1980. *Derek Cross*

Right: As explained in the accompanying text, the definition of 'around London' has been extended somewhat, partly to justify the inclusion of pictures such as this, taken on 10 May 1958. Headed by Brush Type 2 No D5505, then just three months old, arrives at Witham, some 39 miles from Liverpool Street, with a train for Ipswich. Later renumbered 31 005, this locomotive was to enjoy a short spell of fame towards the end of its career, being painted (along with No 31 019) with Stratford depot's trademark silver roof for use on farewell railtours in 1977. *R. C. Riley*

First published 2007

ISBN (10) 0 7110 3083 9
ISBN (13) 978 0 7110 3083 1

© David Cross 2007

Published by Ian Allan Publishing

an imprint of Ian Allan Publishing Ltd, Hersham, Surrey KT12 4RG
Printed in England by Ian Allan Printing Ltd, Hersham, Surrey KT12 4RG

Code 0706/B2

Visit the Ian Allan Publishing website at www.ianallanpublishing.com

Introduction

There can be no doubt that the railway network in and around London is one of the most complex in the world. With 12 major termini, some of which are amongst the most famous stations in the world (four make the original Monopoly game board!), plus freight lines and the extensive Underground network there is a great deal to choose from, and in the 'Sixties and 'Seventies there was exceptional variety in terms of diesel and electric motive power.

In this book I have tried to cover as much variety as possible and hopefully have covered most routes into and out of London. In so doing I have sought help and received most useful photographs from the late Dick Riley, John Edgington and Michael Mensing, to add to those taken by my late father, Derek, and indeed some of the more recent ones by myself. I am, needless to say, most grateful to these other photographers for so kindly helping me put the book together. Sadly, during the time this book has been in preparation Dick Riley died, aged 84. He has left a matchless collection of 'Sixties material in the London area more or less unrivalled in its range of subjects and quality. I am very pleased to have had the use of this material and wish the Transport Treasury every success in sharing the Riley collection with the public.

For fifty years (off and on) my father or I have commuted into London to work. In the late 'Forties Derek, during his final university exams at London University, commuted from Berkhamsted, and he often mentioned that he had found this most frustrating. To be both interested in and a user of the rail network leads to all kinds of dilemmas! He recalled that once on the way to an exam by train into Euston he saw a rare ex-works 'Jubilee' backing down into the station, but as he had both an exam to sit and no camera he had to forgo something he would normally set out deliberately to see and/or photograph. It was much the same after we returned to the UK from New Zealand in the late 'Fifties, when he commuted from West Croydon to Charing Cross, again with a similar dichotomy — work or pleasure?

For the best part of 30 years now I have also commuted into London. Regular journeys from Wolverhampton to Euston (for three months — this being the most ambitious or foolhardy, depending on which way you look at it), from Sutton to London Bridge, from Ongar (now sadly closed) and Stratford on the Underground, from Upminster to Fenchurch Street and from Brentwood and Shenfield on the GE have led to encounters similar to those experienced by Derek all those years ago. An ex-works Class 31 in 'red stripe' Railfreight livery on an express to Norwich comes to mind in much the same way as Derek and his 'Jubilee'!

Derek preferred the train in the landscape, and it has to be said that he much preferred the rural as opposed to industrial or built-up landscape. Perhaps because of this — or perhaps because of the frustration of trying to rationalise his hobby with his journey to work — he did not take many photographs in London, and sadly those he did take tended to be at the same locations, Kenton on the LMR and Hadley Wood and Potters Bar on the ER being among his favourites.

This book covers the period from the late 'Fifties to the early 'Eighties — an era of unrivalled variety in terms of diesel and electric traction in the London area. As the 'Fifties drew to a close a new-look British Railways was emerging, both by design and of necessity with the rapid spread postwar of the private car and the commercial lorry, which were having a significant effect on rail passenger numbers, freight volumes and, of course, revenue. Basically trains had to move faster to remain competitive, and as a consequence the early diesel programme was accelerated. This led to the fleet of fewer than 200 Pilot Scheme diesels being expanded rapidly with a plethora of new and different classes appearing in a rush from a variety of manufacturers. Most of these classes (some of which were successful, others much less so!) all appeared in Greater London at some stage. Some, such as the BRCW and NBL Type 2s on the Great Northern section, stayed only very briefly, but I have included as many as I could find. In so doing I have 'extended' Greater London to take in Ampthill (Bedfordshire) and Witham (Essex).

I am often asked what cameras Derek used. Some of the later material in this book was taken on large format transparencies of 2¼in x 3¼in rectangular negatives with just eight to a 120-size film. Later this changed to 12 negatives of 2¼in square to one 120-size film. The film used was almost exclusively Agfa CT18, and the hardware a Linhof press camera, later replaced by a Rollei SL66, of which he spoke highly. The colour material was taken on Kodachrome II film with a 35mm Leica camera (with interchangeable lenses) or with an early Canon SLR. Through the 1970s film speed improved a great deal, and with faster film it became easier to take colour pictures in poor weather or under London's station roofs! Much of Dick Riley's

material was taken on 35mm with an Agfa Silette camera. My own early-'Seventies material was again on 35mm slides using Kodachrome I film and was taken with a Konica camera.

Finally, I should like to thank my wife for her patience in putting up with this eccentric hobby and the unusual hours, and for her assistance during the production of this book (especially as my handwriting sometimes verges on the illegible!). I do hope you enjoy the result.

David Cross
Brentwood
March 2007

Left: A remarkable view of Waterloo, one of the busiest passenger stations in London, recorded on Saturday 18 June 1983. Unusually, at a terminus where passenger workings predominate, freight/engineers' trains are in the majority. Nearest the camera is a Class 508 electric multiple-unit on a suburban service to Kingston-upon-Thames. The track-laying operation behind features electro-diesel No 73 123 on a train of rails, Class 33 diesel-electric No 33 012 on a ballast train and a Class 09 diesel shunter light-engine. *Author*

Above: In 2006 the 'Blue Pullman' concept was revived for a charter train operated by FM Rail, using air-conditioned Mk 2d/e/f coaching stock 'topped-and-tailed' by a pair of Class 47/7s built by Brush in 1966. Bound for Shoeburyness on the Essex coast, the formation is seen leaving Fenchurch Street in June 2006, with No 47 712 *Artemis* (originally No D1948) leading and No 47 709 *Dionysos* (ex D1942) bringing up the rear. Regrettably the demise of FM Rail at the end of 2006 threw the future of this train into doubt, and it is to be hoped that in due course locomotives and stock will be reunited to allow operation to resume. *Author*

Left: Completed at its builder's Loughborough works just a few days earlier and placed in traffic from Stratford depot, Brush Type 2 No D5516 approaches Liverpool Street station on Thursday 2 October 1958 with the 11.48am express from Ely; above the train can be seen the approach to the adjacent Broad Street (left). The first 20 Brush Type 2s were ordered as part of the Pilot Scheme and, it is said, derived from an order that that the Loughborough builder had recently completed for the Ceylon Government Railway; fitted with 1,250hp Mirrless engines, they would be followed by a further 243 machines with engines uprated to 1,365hp. In the years 1965-9 all would be re-engined with English Electric power units rated at 1,470hp (becoming Class 31), but the first 20, always based on the GE section, were regarded as non-standard on account of their 'toffee-apple' control equipment and would all be withdrawn by the end of 1980. Renumbered 31 016 in May 1974, this example would continue to be based at Stratford for its entire career, which was to end in July 1976. *R. C. Riley*

Above: For years Liverpool Street station was rather a gloomy place, and this picture, taken in July 1970, serves to confirm the point! The station, which had replaced Shoreditch as the Great Eastern Railway's principal London terminus *c*1874, was built in two parts. The west side (today's Platforms 1-10) was opened first, the east side (Platforms 11-18) being added about 20 years later. Extensively rebuilt in the 1990s, the station is now bright and airy and is one of the most impressive of the London termini. Still with 18 platforms, it is now one of the capital's busiest stations, handling around a million passengers per week. Back in July 1970 the station pilot, concerning itself with both releasing main-line locomotives and shunting parcels and mail vans, was BTH/Clayton Type 1 No D8234. The concept of station pilots is now long gone, as is No D8234, which had an active career of just 11 years (1960-71) and was always based at nearby Stratford depot. Sister locomotive No D8233 is preserved at Bury on the East Lancashire Railway and is expected to return to working order in 2008. *Author*

The last day of February 1959 finds English Electric Type 4 No D205 approaching Bethnal Green station, 1½ miles from Liverpool Street, with an express for Norwich, some 124 miles distant. The route was the first main line in the country to become diesel-operated, these 2,000hp machines having replaced steam on the long-distance services to and from Liverpool Street in the late 1950s. Their tenure would be short, however, for by the late 1960s they would be replaced on such work by the more powerful Brush/Sulzer Type 4 (Class 47) locomotives. Built at Vulcan Foundry in May 1958, No D205 was to remain in traffic (latterly as No 40 005) until early 1976, becoming one of the first Class 40s to be scrapped, at Crewe in February 1977. *R. C. Riley*

Seen at the same location on the same day is Brush Type 2 No D5514 heading the 12.0 service from King's Cross to King's Lynn, which train included through carriages for Hunstanton. Placed in traffic in July 1958 from Stratford, this locomotive would remain allocated to that depot, latterly as No 31 014, until withdrawal in 1976, thereafter enjoying a number of years' stay of execution as a carriage-heating vehicle. *R. C. Riley*

Left: The diamond-shaped NB plate immediately identifying the Glasgow-based manufacturer, a pair of North British Type 1 diesels rest in the sidings at Stratford diesel depot (then still coded 30A) between duties on Thursday 7 June 1959. Built in 1958 and fitted with 800hp Paxman engines, the 10 locomotives of this unsuccessful class spent almost all of their short lives on transfer freights and shunting in London's East End. Designated Class 16 under TOPS, they would all be withdrawn long before the implementation of the renumbering scheme. No D8406, completed in September 1958, would be among the last to remain in traffic, being condemned after a working life of exactly 10 years. *R. C. Riley*

Below left: Thursday 7 June 1959 finds English Electric 500hp 0-6-0 diesel-hydraulic shunter No D227 on shed at Stratford. Not to be confused with the English Electric Type 4s carrying the same number, this locomotive and diesel-electric sister No D226 had been built speculatively by English Electric at the famous Vulcan Foundry at Newton-le-Willows in 1956 and loaned to British Railways with a view to gaining bulk orders. Both allocated initially to Stratford (and later renumbered as D0226/7 to avoid confusion with similarly numbered EE Type 4s), the pair lasted in BR stock for only a very short time, No D0227 being withdrawn from Bristol St Philips Marsh in October 1960. No D0226 survives in preservation at Haworth on the Keighley & Worth Valley Railway. *R. C. Riley*

Right: Always an interesting place, Stratford depot was once home to hundreds of diesel locomotives, and often 50 or more would be on shed at any one time. In the days before excessive Health & Safety legislation shed staff conducted a guided tour of the shed every Saturday morning; having gathered in the dark, damp tunnel underneath the passenger station the group would be treated to the sight of row upon row of locomotives on shed and in the works — a veritable Aladdin's Cave, all for the princely sum of 50 pence. Those were the days! This photograph, taken on the afternoon of 14 July 1979, depicts a Class 15, formerly No D8243, which by this time was in departmental stock as mobile carriage-heating unit No ADB968000. Numerically the last of this class of 44 800hp BTH/Clayton locomotives, it had been withdrawn from traffic as early as February 1969. *R. C. Riley*

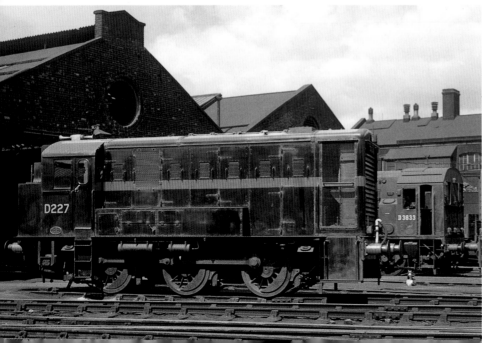

Left: Stratford Works was for years associated mainly with diesels that worked on the GE lines out of Liverpool Street. However, as the number of other locomotive workshops was reduced it saw a much greater variety of locomotives. Pictured here in August 1982 are locomotives of four different classes — 24, 31, 46 and 47 — most prominent being Nos 46 004 and 24 142 (by now in departmental stock as No TDB968009). Both are at Stratford for repairs, perhaps having failed in the London area. No 46 004, turned out by Crewe Works in November 1961 as No D141, was by this time allocated to Gateshead depot, from which it would be withdrawn 10 months later. Completed at Derby in November 1960 as No D5142, No 24 142 had been taken out of traffic in July 1976 but was retained in Departmental service as a carriage-heating vehicle, initially at Exeter, finally being withdrawn in September 1982. *Author*

Above: The autumn of 1981 — 27 October, to be precise — finds Class 31/1 No 31 216 passing through Stratford station *en route* to Liverpool Street with an express from Harwich Parkeston Quay, where in all likelihood it would have connected with a ferry sailing from Hook of Holland; worked by electric units, such boat trains still run to/from Harwich today. The locomotive had been completed by Brush in August 1960 as No D5641 and allocated new to Finsbury Park depot; upon conversion in 1985 to provide electric train heating it would be renumbered again as 31 467, in which guise it would be withdrawn in March 1998. It currently awaits restoration at Bury, on the East Lancashire Railway. *Author*

Pictured on 31 March 1962, Brush Type 2 No D5588 passes Abbey Mills Junction (near Canning Town, in London's East End) with a goods for the North Woolwich branch, while lurking behind the substantial signalbox is a brand-new English Electric Type 3. Much of the goods traffic at this time was to and from the London Docks, which with the advent of containerisation would move downriver to Tilbury by the early 'Seventies. In 1973 No D5588 would be renumbered as 31 170, in which guise it would be withdrawn from Immingham depot in January 1990. *R. C. Riley*

Another view of the large and imposing signalbox at Abbey Mills Junction, this time with BTH Type 1 No D8229 working a transfer freight in March 1962. Completed in June 1960 as one of a class of 44 and allocated initially to Ipswich shed, this locomotive, in common with its sisters, would see barely 10 years' service, being withdrawn from Stratford depot in March 1971. *R. C. Riley*

In the depths of the East End on a wet afternoon in March 1963 we find diesel shunter No D4192 on the Silvertown tramway, which ran from Thames Wharf Junction (near Canning Town) via a swing bridge to Silvertown. The train is an RCTS brake-van tour of essentially freight-only branches, of which there were literally hundreds in the area, all associated with the nearby London Docks. Run by the Port of London Authority, the Docks had an extensive railway network of their own which met with the then British Railways at several points in this area. No D4192 was the last diesel shunter built by BR, at Darlington Works, in September 1962, just six months before this photograph was taken. Renumbered 08 958 in 1974, it would have a long career working along the Thames, finally being withdrawn from Stratford in December 1993. *John Edgington*

Pictured on the branch to North Woolwich in London's Docklands in April 1984 (before they became fashionable!) is an F&W railtour from North Woolwich to Plymouth headed by Class 37s Nos 37 038 and 37 089. A Class 50, still attached at the rear, had hauled the train to the terminus of North Woolwich, and these two freight machines had been attached to drag the train back to Temple Mills yard. At that time the passenger service on this line was DMU-worked, the pick-up goods normally seeing a Class 31. The passenger services is no longer operating and will be replaced in due course by an extension of the DLR. There is no longer any freight, but the 'Royal Albert' pub (visible here in the background) gives a clue as to the area's industrial past, the Royal Albert and Queen Victoria docks having been amongst the largest on the River Thames before containerisation swept away the conventional ships and their port downstream to Tilbury. Built by Robert Stephenson & Hawthorn subsidiary in January 1963 as No D6789, No 37 089 would be rebuilt in 1988 as Class 37/7 heavy-freight locomotive No 37 708, being withdrawn in October 2002; turned out by Vulcan Foundry in May 1962 as No D6738, No 37 038 remains in service in more-or-less original condition with Direct Rail Services. *Author*

Left: Saturday 17 September 1977 finds a number of locomotives lined up in the shed area at the purpose-built Ripple Lane servicing depot. A subshed of Stratford located just east of Barking on the Tilbury loop, this provided motive power for the multiplicity of oil trains travelling to and from the large oil refinery at Shellhaven, near Stanford-le-Hope. Pictured here are Class 31/1 No 31 156, turned out by Brush in December 1959 as No D5574, and Class 37 No 37 057, completed by English Electric in October 1962 as No D6757. The former would be withdrawn in August 1991, the latter, subsequently named *Viking*, being stood down by EWS as recently as October 2004. *Author*

Below: Still in green livery, Class 08 No 08 494 stands at Ripple Lane in September 1977. Built at Horwich Works in March 1958 as No D3609, this 350hp shunter would remain in traffic until August 1988, being scrapped three years later by MC Metals of Glasgow. Ripple Lane depot also is no more, the site now being occupied by a breaker's yard. *Author*

Containerisation in the 1970s saw the bulk of traffic to/from London Docks move 20 miles downriver to Tilbury, the Thames not being navigable by the larger vessels now required. Illuminated by weak winter sunshine on 25 January 1984, a pair of Class 37s perpare their Freightliner train for departure for Coatbridge in Scotland. Built by Vulcan Foundry, Nos 37 044 and 37 047 had entered traffic (as Nos D6744 and D6747) from Sheffield's Darnall shed within a month of each other in the summer of 1962 and would both be stood down by EWS (the former having been rebuilt in February 1988 as Class 37/7 No 37 710) in January 2005. *Author*

King's Cross on the afternoon of 6 September 1971 finds blue 'Deltic' No 9014 *The Duke of Wellington's Regiment* and green-liveried Brush Type 2 No D5590 about to set off with northbound passenger services. Post Office trolleys and what appears to be a loading ramp of some kind litter the platforms, confirming that in those days parcels and mail traffic was an important feature of all the large London termini. As well as this platform furniture such traffic called for a much greater variety of stock and motive power than can be seen today at these essentially passenger-only stations. The early 'Seventies also saw a great variety of liveries with the ongoing changeover from green to blue, with lots of exceptions and unusual liveries as with No D5590 here, with full yellow ends but still with the old BR logo. Renumbered 31 171, this locomotive would remain in service until October 1993, but the 'Deltic', latterly No 55 014, would be withdrawn from York in November 1981. *R. C. Riley*

A scene, recorded on 6 September 1971 from the end of Platform 8 at King's Cross, that will doubtless be familiar to many readers. On the left are a pair of Class 47s and, in the F&I (fuel and inspection) shed, Gateshead-allocated Class 46 'Peak' No D193, while nearest the camera is Class 31 No D5647, arriving with a train of empty carriage stock.

Renumbered 46 056, the 'Peak' would be withdrawn in October 1982, the Class 31 surviving, latterly as No 31 221, until August 1991. Sadly the King's Cross shed area would find itself redundant in the era of multiple-units and is now occupied by a car park. *R. C. Riley*

21

Above: One of a class of 10 built at Vulcan Foundry in the spring of 1959, English Electric Type 2 No D5906 appears to be making reasonable progress up the 1-in-107 gradient past Belle Isle as it accelerates away from King's Cross with the 10.30am service for Cambridge on 18 March 1961. Regrettably these locomotives, nicknamed 'Baby Deltics' on account of their single Napier Deltic engines, were not a great success; only two would last in service into the 'Seventies, No D5906 being withdrawn in September 1968. *R. C. Riley*

Right: Headed by Brush Type 2 No D5674, the empty stock from the 'Queen of Scots' Pullman service from Edinburgh is removed from King's Cross for cleaning and servicing at the nearby carriage sidings, the train being pictured at Belle Isle. In the foreground is confirmation that this picture, taken in 1961, dates from the steam era, with a diesel shunter preparing a number of coal wagons for the Gresley Pacifics that still worked the East Coast main line at this time. *R. C. Riley*

One for the modeller, perhaps, with great detail of the signals, signalbox, trackside furniture (including an outside workbench, complete with vice!) and the mouth of Copenhagen Tunnel. Brake No SC16356E is the leading vehicle in a train of empty carriage stock from King's Cross to the sidings at Hornsey or Ferme Park. The photograph was taken on 18 March 1961, at which time Brush Type 2 locomotive No D5677, completed in December 1960, was just three months old; later renumbered 31 249, it would remain in traffic until December 1991. *R. C. Riley*

On a beautifully sunny 18 March 1961 Brush Type 2 No D5679 emerges from Copenhagen Tunnel, just over a mile from King's Cross, at the head of an outer-suburban service from Baldock. The semaphores, the signalbox, the locomotive's green livery and the 'quad-art' set all contribute to a memorable picture that captures perfectly the transition from the steam age to the modern era. New in December 1960, No D5679 would be renumbered as 31 251 and again (upon conversion in 1984 to provide electric train heating) as 31 442, in which guise it would be withdrawn in September 1993. *R. C. Riley*

Left: The suburban stations at the southern end of the East Coast main line come thick and fast, there being no fewer than 15 in the 32 miles between Hitchin and King's Cross. One such, eight miles from the London terminus, is Oakleigh Park, visible in the background, beyond the DMU, as Brush Type 2 No D5602 heads south with a train from Royston. The photograph was taken in July 1960, at which time the locomotive was just three months old; latterly numbered 31 181, it was to remain in service for a further 35 years. *Derek Cross*

Below left: Derek and his contemporaries did us all a favour by taking pictures such as this back in 1960. This might seem a strange comment, but often, when they had turned out to record an 'A4' or 'A3' Pacific and a diesel came into view, they did not take the shot at all! Luckily this Edinburgh Waverley–King's Cross express was recorded approaching Oakleigh Park Tunnel behind English Electric Type 4 No D247. New to Gateshead depot (52A) late in 1959 and put to work on East Coast expresses such as this, the locomotive would gradually be 'cascaded' as more powerful locomotives came into service. Later renumbered 40 047, it was to remain in traffic for nearly 25 years, eventually being withdrawn in November 1984 from Longsight depot in Manchester. *Derek Cross*

The English Electric 3,300hp *Deltic* prototype races towards Oakleigh Park Tunnel with a Hull–King's Cross service in the summer of 1960. Built at the Dick Kerr works in Preston in 1955 and based originally on the London Midland Region, it was transferred in January 1959 to the Eastern Region at Hornsey, where its performance was sufficiently impressive to prompt an order for 22 production machines. Its job done, it was retired in March 1961 and placed on static display at the Science Museum at South Kensington; later transferred to the National Railway Museum, it is now based at the latter's annexe at Shildon, County Durham. For the benefit of readers wondering why this is a 'going away' shot it should perhaps be explained that Derek would often take a black-and-white picture of a train as it approached and a colour one after it had passed! *Derek Cross*

Above: Only eight months old, having been placed in traffic in October 1958 from Hornsey shed, BRCW/Sulzer Type 2 No D5302 hurries south near Hadley Wood in the summer of 1959 with an up local formed of a 'quad-art' set. In the background, beyond the last carriage (and contrasting with the blackened entrance of the original bore to the right), can be seen the new tunnel constructed upon quadrupling of the East Coast main line, while the spotters' bicycles and simple gate crossing (left) are typical of the era. In the late 1950s new diesels of different classes were introduced to replace ageing steam locomotives on the GN suburban services to/from King's Cross, but none save the Brush Type 2s stayed for any length of time; No D5302 would be transferred the following year to Scotland, where (latterly as No 26 002) it was to spend the rest of its working life. *Derek Cross*

Right: For a brief period the first NBL Type 2s were allocated to Hornsey (34B) for use on semi-fast services from King's Cross. This photograph, taken in August 1959, features No D6102 approaching Hadley Wood with a train from Cambridge, including what appears to be a full restaurant car in a mixed rake of rolling stock. Also of note are the semaphore signals in the distance. By early 1960, following a succession of failures with its early diesels, BR had decided that these technical difficulties would be best solved by concentrating particular classes in particular areas. The NBL Type 2 diesel-electrics were all transferred to Scotland, where they had been built, it being felt that the mechanical problems from which they were suffering would be most easily addressed if they were close to the NBL works in Glasgow. In 1965 No D6102 would be one of an eventual 20 locomotives from this class of 58 to have its original MAN engine replaced by a Paxman unit, in which form (known latterly as Class 29) it would be finally be withdrawn in October 1971 from Eastfield depot in Glasgow. *Derek Cross*

New in December 1960 from the famous Falcon Works in Loughborough, Brush Type 2 No D5674 had been in traffic for eight months when pictured at Ganwick *en route* to the capital. The train is 2B65, a Baldock–King's Cross semi-fast, the next stop in all likelihood Finsbury Park, eight miles distant. No D5674 would be renumbered in February 1974 as 31 246 and again in November 1984 as 31 455, in which guise it would be withdrawn in September 1996. *Derek Cross*

English Electric Type 4 No D257 bursts out of the tunnel at Ganwick (just north of Hadley Wood) with a King's Cross–Newcastle express on 13 June 1961. The majority of these 136-ton 2,000hp machines, of which some 200 were built in the years 1958-62, were used to replace steam on expresses from Liverpool Street, Euston and King's Cross, but as the 'Sixties progressed they were relegated to secondary services and ultimately freight.

All but one of these locomotives, known latterly Class 40s, would be withdrawn by 1985; new to York shed in February 1960, this example (latterly numbered 40 057) was to end its career in July 1984 at Manchester's Longsight depot. Sister locomotives Nos D200/12/3, 306/18/35/45 survive in preservation. *Derek Cross*

Pictured on 19 June 1959, just five months after entering service at Hornsey depot (34B), 1,160hp BRCW/Sulzer Type 2 No D5317 storms away from Potters Bar station with a train from King's Cross to Baldock in Hertfordshire — a journey of 37 miles. Built at Smethwick, near Birmingham, between July 1958 and March 1959, the first 20 members of this class were allocated from new to ER London-suburban duties but did not stay for long, all being transferred within a year or so to Scotland, where they joined a further 27 of the type delivered later in 1959 and spent the remainder of their working lives, doing sterling service, particularly on the Highland and Far North lines. No fewer than 13 members of the class survive in preservation. *Derek Cross*

Right: In a wonderful 'Fifties scene that epitomises what this book is all about a North British Type 2 heads a set of 'quad-arts' past Potters Bar on a commuter service from King's Cross to Hitchin. Completed by NBL in Glasgow in December 1958, No D6102 was allocated to Hornsey depot in London for use on the Great Northern section. The picture was taken in June 1959 — and just as well, because by February 1960 this locomotive would be stored unserviceable after only 14 months in traffic. Reinstated later in the year, it was soon transferred to Scotland, where it saw service in the Glasgow area and on the West Highland lines. Rebuilding in 1965 with a Paxman engine at least ensured its survival into the 'Seventies (until October 1971, to be precise), most unrebuilt locomotives being withdrawn as early as 1967. *Derek Cross*

Right: Recorded in August 1959, another suburban service from King's Cross to Baldock accelerates away from the Potters Bar stop behind BRCW/Sulzer Type 2 No D5303. The next stop will be Brookmans Park, then Hatfield and Welwyn *en route* to the junction for Baldock at Hitchin. The variety of diesel locomotives on GN suburban services at this time was enormous, although the Brush Type 2s would soon make these services their own and would remain the staple motive power until electrification in 1976. By contrast No D5303, placed in traffic at Hornsey depot in October 1958, was to stay for barely a year before being transferred to Scotland, where Derek would photograph it still at work 25 years later. *Derek Cross*

Left: Saturday 14 April 1984 saw Luton Town Football Club play Tottenham Hotspur FC in a League match at White Hart Lane. At a time when car ownership was less widespread (and when there was sufficient surplus rolling stock) 'Footex' specials were still commonplace, and this picture, taken at Crouch Hill, between Gospel Oak and South Tottenham on the North London line, shows one of two specials run that day from Luton to North London, a relatively short distance of about 40 miles. Motive power was provided by Class 47/4 No 47 418, a long-term ECML performer; completed by Brush in April 1963 as No D1517 and placed in traffic from Finsbury Park, it would be withdrawn from Gateshead in February 1991. For those interested in football, 'Spurs' won the match 2-1! *Author*

Above: Some of the final Class 104 BRCW DMUs in passenger service with British Rail spent their last few years plying between Gospel Oak and Barking. In this picture, taken in May 1984, a two-car set arrives at Crouch Hill *en route* for Gospel Oak. At the time allocated to Bletchley, these units would remain in traffic (latterly from Old Oak Common) until ousted by Class 117 DMUs, themselves displaced from Paddington by new Class 165 'Networkers'. *Author*

Left: Pictured leaving St Pancras in the autumn of 1962 is one of the two six-car 'Midland Pullman' diesel units built by Metro-Cammell. On the right of the picture can be seen the famous gas-holders, recently dismantled and placed in store with the promise that at least one of them will return once the work associated with converting the station for Channel Tunnel services has been completed. *John Edgington*

Below left: One of the 'Midland Pullman' sets awaiting departure. Introduced from the 1960 summer timetable, these units worked between St Pancras and Manchester Central via the Midland main line, but electrification in 1966 of the West Coast main line would allow the 'Manchester Pullman' between Euston and Manchester Piccadilly a faster journey time, the two 'Midland Pullman' units then being transferred to the Western region, where they were to remain in service until 1973. *R. C. Riley*

Right: The size and splendour of William Barlow's magnificent trainshed at St Pancras are evident in this 1983 picture of Class 45/1 No 45 131 arriving with an afternoon service from Derby. By this time locomotive-hauled expresses on the Midland main line were beginning to give way to High Speed Trains, one of which can be seen in the background prior to departing for Sheffield. Turned out by Crewe Works in November 1961 as No D124, the 'Peak' would remain in traffic until March 1985. *Author*

An afternoon in May 1970 finds two BR/Sulzer Type 4 'Peaks' at the country end of St Pancras station, originally the London terminus of the erstwhile Midland Railway. On the left Derby-built No 144 (by this time the 'D' prefix was beginning to disappear), which would later be renumbered 46 007, is on the Sheffield service, while on the right Crewe-built No D117 (later No 45 130) waits to depart for Nottingham. The large maroon-and-white station nameboard identifies the London Midland Region (LMR) of British Railways. *Author*

A visit to St Pancras on the afternoon of 10 May 1983 finds the then usual fare of 'Peaks'. On the left is Class 45/1 No 45 133 about to depart with the 15.30 London–Nottingham service, whilst in the foreground is sister No 45 127 at the head of the 15.24 London–Derby, both trains being formed of air-conditioned Mark 2d/e/f stock in blue and grey. Both locomotives would be made redundant from the Midland main line by the advent of High Speed Trains. No 45 133, turned out by Derby Works in July 1961 as No D40, is now preserved at the Midland Railway Centre at Butterley, Derbyshire; No 45 127, completed by Crewe in February 1961 as No D87, would be less fortunate, being withdrawn in May 1987 and scrapped at its birthplace in March 1994. *Author*

Left: Pictured near Leagrave, some 33 miles from the start of its journey on the Midland main line from St Pancras, 'Peak' No D71 hurries a London–Sheffield service northwards in June 1965. Although perhaps one of the less fashionable lines to/from London, the Midland main line saw the 'Peaks' for years turn in some first-class performances on quite demanding schedules to Derby, Nottingham, Leeds, Sheffield and Glasgow. Turned out by Crewe Works in November 1960, this locomotive, named in 1966 as *The Staffordshire Regiment (The Prince of Wales's)*, would be renumbered 45 049 in 1975 and remain in traffic until February 1988. *Michael Mensing*

Below left: Bound for London with an express from Nottingham, 'Peak' No D126 races through the Bedfordshire countryside near Ampthill in June 1965. Some 42 miles from St Pancras, the Midland main line at this point consists of four tracks, the fast lines being the two nearest the camera. The 'Peaks', with a 1Co-Co1 wheel arrangement, were large (67ft 11in long) and, at 133 tons, heavy locomotives. Having been equipped to provide electric train heating, No D126 would be renumbered in 1974 as 45 134, eventually being withdrawn from Tinsley depot in Sheffield in September 1987. *Michael Mensing*

Right: Formed of a four-car Derby DMU, train 2C59, a semi-fast service from Bedford to St Pancras, is 8 miles into its journey as it emerges from Ampthill Tunnel in May 1965. These DMUs would provide the commuter service for many years, until electrification of the line between Bedford and Moorgate in May 1982. Since the photograph was taken the station at the small market town of Ampthill, has closed, passengers now being directed to use the station at Flitwick, some 2 miles to the south. Just out of sight on the right is Houghton House. Designed by Inigo Jones and built in 1615, this was reputedly the model for the 'House Beautiful' in John Bunyan's *The Pilgrim's Progress*. Empty since 1935, the pollution from several nearby brickworks having eroded much of the stonework, it is presently being restored by English Heritage. *Michael Mensing*

Right: 'Peak' No D134 hurries a St Pancras–Nottingham service through rural Bedfordshire near Ampthill in June 1965. New in December 1961 to Derby shed (17A), the locomotive had taken on a distinctly careworn appearance in the intervening three years. Renumbered 45 076 in January 1975, it would remain in traffic until the end of 1986. *Michael Mensing*

Left: Having recently arrived with an express from the North West, an unidentified English Electric Type 4 stands alongside rebuilt 'Royal Scot' No 46155 *The Lancer*, then of Crewe North shed, at Euston in 1961. The EE Type 4s worked with and gradually took over from steam on the main passenger turns to and from Euston from 1959. However, their reign was to be short, as by 1966 Euston station would be rebuilt, and both steam and diesel banished northwards in favour of electric locomotives. *John Edgington*

Above: Photographed in March 1963, English Electric 2,700hp diesel prototype No DP2 prepares to leave Euston with the 1.35pm service to Perth. Having entered service in the spring of 1962, it would remain on the LMR for 15 months or so before being returned to the manufacturer and used thereafter on the East Coast main line, ultimately being written off in an accident near Thirsk in 1967. Although it looked like a 'Deltic' it was more closely related to the EE Type 3s and Type 4s, and indeed many of its features would be incorporated in the later EE Type 4 (Class 50) locomotives built at Vulcan Foundry in 1967/8. *John Edgington*

Nowadays the appearance of a locomotive at Euston is regarded as something of an event, while a station pilot anywhere is more-or-less unknown. However, back in April 1972, Class 25 No 7658 was busying itself drawing empty coaching stock out of the platform, either to release the electric locomotive that had brought the train in or to take the empty stock for servicing. Watching proceedings from another platform is Class 86 electric locomotive No E3142 waiting to depart with a Manchester express.

Built at Gorton, Manchester, by Beyer Peacock, No 7658 had been introduced to traffic as D7658 in July 1966 and allocated to the LMR's London division; subsequently renumbered 25 308, it would be withdrawn from Toton in October 1983 after a mere 17 years' service. Completed in February 1966 at Vulcan Foundry, the electric would be renumbered 86 254 (after a brief period as 86 047) and later named *William Webb Ellis*, remaining in service thus until October 2002. *Author*

The turntable on the left helps identify the location as being close to a large steam shed, in this case Camden (1B), just two miles north of Euston station, and indeed the picture was taken, on 3 June 1962, from the shed's coaling tower. The train, a Northampton–Euston semi-fast headed by 1,160hp BR/Sulzer Type 2 No D5146, is passing Primrose Hill station. New to nearby Willesden depot (1A) in December 1960, this Derby-built locomotive, renumbered 24 146 in March 1974, would be withdrawn in January 1976 from Crewe. *R. C. Riley*

Above: Headed by English Electric Type 1s Nos D8000 and D8003, a short freight, in all likelihood destined for the extensive yard complex between Wembley and Willesden, passes beneath the ex-Great Central Aylesbury line at South Kenton in June 1958. Allocated to British Railways' first purpose-built diesel depot, at Devons Road, Bow (1D, later 1J), both locomotives were from the initial batch of 20 delivered as part of the Pilot Scheme. New to traffic in August 1957, No D8003 would be withdrawn in December 1982 as No 20 003, succumbing to the scrapman at Crewe Works in January 1984. Fortunately a happier fate awaited No D8000, new in June 1957: withdrawn in December 1980 after a period of relative obscurity as No 20 050, this historic locomotive — BR's first production main-line diesel — now resides at the National Railway Museum at York, where it will celebrate its 50th birthday in the summer of 2007. *Derek Cross*

Above right: Having completed 183 miles of its 193-mile journey, the up 'Merseyside Express' from Liverpool Lime Street to Euston approaches Kenton in July 1960. In the foreground are the DC suburban lines shared

as far as Watford by British Railways and London Transport's Bakerloo Line. Complete with headboard, the train, consisting of 14 coaches and a covered carriage truck is hauled by an English Electric Type 4 from the D210-236 series, new to the LMR the previous year. *Derek Cross*

Right: Also photographed near Kenton, some 10 miles from its destination, was this semi-fast service from Northampton in June 1960. The locomotive, No 10203, was one of three 1Co-Co1 diesel-electrics built by BR's Southern Region at Ashford in 1950/1 (10201/2) or Brighton in 1954 (10203). Trialled on the SR and on the Midland main line, they did not make the necessary impact to lead to a full production run. By the end of 1955 all three had been reallocated to Camden shed to work on the West Coast main line. Nos 10201 and 10202 tended to work as a pair, the more powerful No 10203 (2,000hp compared to 1,600hp) generally operating on its own. All three would be withdrawn by the end of 1963, ultimately being scrapped by Cashmore's at Great Bridge in January 1968. *Derek Cross*

Forming a suburban service to Aylesbury, some 38 miles away, a Class 115 DMU makes a typically smoky exit from Marylebone station on Saturday 14 April 1984. Less common at a station which for more than 40 years now has been the preserve of DMUs is Class 50 No 50 040, at that time named *Leviathan* (but which, unusually for a Class 50, would be renamed in 1987 as *Centurion*, a name it was to carry until withdrawal in July 1990). Its presence here is explained by the fact that it was awaiting the arrival of the F&W Railtours excursion from Plymouth (featured opposite) before taking that train forward to North Woolwich. *Author*

Shortly after the previous picture was taken the F&W railtour from Plymouth arrived at Marylebone behind Class 25s Nos 25 042 and 25 083. The train had left the Devon city at the unearthly hour of 04.13, but, judging from the well-filled 12-coach rake of Mk 1 stock, this was no deterrent to the participants! Both locomotives had been turned out by BR's Derby Works in 1963, in May and December respectively as Nos D5192 and D5233. No 25 042 would be withdrawn in 1986 and cut up in 1987 at Vic Berry's Leicester yard, but No 25 083, after a somewhat Houdini-like existence following withdrawal in 1984, has now found a secure home at Brechin on the Caledonian Railway, where a return to service is expected later in 2007. *Author*

Above: Beneath the roof of Brunel's famous trainshed at Paddington in the spring of 1961 the white-capped driver of the 'Bristol Pullman' checks that his unit is ready to depart. As its name suggests, the train was an express from London Paddington to Bristol Temple Meads, conveying First-class passengers in Pullman luxury. Built by Metro-Cammell in Birmingham in 1960, the 'Blue Pullman' units were shared by the London Midland and Western regions, the WR sets being put to work on services to the West Midlands and to Bristol. The Midlands service would be withdrawn in 1966, that to/from Bristol surviving until May 1973. *John Edgington*

Right: Having just disembarked from train 1A99, an express from Oxford, passengers hurry past Class 31/1 No 31 259 at Paddington's Platform 1 in June 1974. Over the years the Oxford services have seen a number of changes between diesel multiple-units and loco-hauled trains. Following the demise of steam, Swindon-built 'Inter-City' DMUs held sway before giving way to loco-hauled trains, with Class 50s and Class 47s, before new, more reliable DMUs took over in the early 1990s. Turned out by Brush as No D5687 in February 1961, No 31 259 would be withdrawn from Tinsley depot in Sheffield in March 1989. This class of 263 locomotives took about five years to build, between 1957 and 1962, but withdrawal, which began in earnest in 1987, has taken four times as long, a number of these veterans remaining active in 2007. *Author*

Right: Thousands of people must have walked past scenes like this at Paddington without taking any notice at all! Luckily in June 1974 Derek was on hand to record a 'Western' hydraulic and a Brush Type 4 at the end of their respective journeys at Platforms 9 and 10. Train 1A97 has arrived from the South West behind 'Western' No 1070 *Western Gauntlet*, whilst 1V11 was an inter-regional working from Birmingham, which had arrived behind Class 47/0 No 47 059, formerly No D1643. By now *Western Gauntlet* had just 18 months left in traffic, whilst 47 059 would go on to become 47 631 and then 47 765, in which guise it was to continue in service into the 21st century before being retired for preservation at Nottingham Heritage Centre.
Derek Cross

'Western' diesel-hydraulic No D1038 *Western Sovereign* arrives at Paddington with train 1A39 from Plymouth. The picture was taken on 19 June 1972 during the author's first solo photographic expedition to London. At that time there was so much to see and photograph that far too long was spent travelling on the Underground between Paddington, Euston, St Pancras, King's Cross and Liverpool Street in pursuit of the great variety of motive power that graced expresses to and from the capital. Built at Crewe in 1962, *Western Sovereign* would remain in traffic only until October 1973, being retired after just 11 years' service. *Author*

Tuesday 15 July 1975 finds train 1B30, a Weston-super-Mare express, at the platform at Paddington waiting to depart at the beginning of its 139-mile journey to the West. Little could it have been realised at the time that prototype unit No 252 001 would be the forerunner of the squadron of HSTs which still today link the West Country with London. Power car No 43001 would be scrapped in 1990, but the car at the other end of the set (No 43000) is now preserved at York as part of the National Collection. *Author*

Left: Class 47/4 No 47 559 *Sir Joshua Reynolds* creeps into Paddington on 25 September 1983 with the 11.45 from Oxford. At this time Class 47s and Class 50s were the regular motive power on these important and busy services, made up of a mixture of Mk 2a/b/c and air-conditioned Mk 2d/e/f coaching stock; the '47/4' classification indicated a locomotive capable of providing electric train heating (ETH), so supplying heating or air-conditioning to these coaches would have presented no problem. Delivered from Crewe Works to Landore (87E) as No D1605 in July 1964, this locomotive had been renumbered 47 028 in 1974 and again as 47 559 upon ETH conversion in November 1980, being named in April 1982. Later it was to become a Parcels-sector locomotive as No 47 759, in which guise it would be withdrawn in January 2003. *Author*

Above: Three InterCity 125 power cars in original livery stand at consecutive platforms at the 'country' end of Paddington station in September 1983. That nearest the camera is No 43026; new in August 1976 and named *City of Westminster* in 1985, it can still be seen today at Paddington on services to the West. The HST, in service now for 30 years, has been a great success all over the country: the 197 lightweight power cars, with a high power-to-weight ratio (2,250hp from 70 tons), were built between 1976 and 1982 at Crewe and have stood the test of time very well. At the time of writing they are undergoing major refurbishment, which will prolong their lives well into the second decade of the 21st century. *Author*

Left: The oldest picture in this book features Western Region single parcels car No W34W leaving Paddington on 30 March 1957. The date is emphasised by the fact that all the locomotives in the background are steam engines; not until the following year would the WR's first main-line diesel locomotives — North British A1A-A1A 'Warships' — make an appearance. The spotters on the left, standing at the end of the platform at Westbourne Park station, appear only slightly interested in the passing of the diesel car, but its crew, both smiling, seem very pleased to be having their photograph taken. *R. C. Riley*

Above: Train 1F86, an express from Paddington to Swansea (the 'F' denoted South Wales destinations), sets off from the famous London terminus at the start of its 191-mile journey on 19 August 1963. The train, which would take more than four hours to reach Swansea (compared with the sub-three-hour times achieved by today's HSTs) is headed by 'Western' diesel-hydraulic No D1042 *Western Princess*. Built at Crewe and placed in traffic in October 1962 from Old Oak Common, this locomotive would be withdrawn from Laira depot in Plymouth in July 1973. *R. C. Riley*

Above: The down 'Torbay Express' sets off from Paddington station on its 208½-mile journey to Kingswear behind the second member of the Swindon-built 'Warship' class, No D801 *Vanguard.* The coaching stock, as might be expected of this prestigious named train, is a matching set of BR Western Region chocolate-and-cream coaches, including a restaurant car. This early diesel-hydraulic locomotive was to see just 10 years' service, being withdrawn in August 1968. The picture was taken on 13 August 1960. *R. C. Riley*

Above right: Pictured in the afternoon sunshine of Saturday 11 April 1964, a pair of 'Western' hydraulics stand outside Old Oak Common shed On the right can be seen the first of the class, No D1000 *Western Enterprise,* in its unique livery of desert sand, whilst on the left, in maroon, is No D1023 *Western Fusilier.* Inevitably on the Western Region at that time there is a supporting cast of a couple of green 'Hymeks' outside the depot. No D1023 is now

preserved as part of the National Collection, nominally based at the NRM in York. *Western Enterprise* would not be so lucky, being cut up at Swindon in July 1974, just five months after withdrawal from Plymouth Laira, although its cast nameplates and numberplates survive on display at the excellent 'Steam' museum in Swindon. *R. C. Riley*

Right: A photograph of a power car of one of the Western Region's three eight-car 'Blue Pullman' sets, taken at Old Oak Common on 10 September 1960 and showing in detail the special livery applied to these prestigious new diesel multiple-units, built in Birmingham by Metro-Cammell. In terms of appearance, speed and levels of comfort they represented a substantial improvement over earlier attempts at luxury travel, and it was a shame that they should remain in service for only around 12 years. *R. C. Riley*

Above left: Just two minutes from journey's end, 'Western' No D1059 *Western Empire* passes the large West London wagonload-freight terminal on the approach to Paddington on 19 October 1963. A through service from Birkenhead via Chester, Shrewsbury, Wolverhampton and Oxford, the train comprises a mixed rake of maroon coaching stock of various origins. Fitted with twin Maybach engines capable of producing a total of 2,700hp, *Western Empire* had been in traffic for only six months. Released from Crewe Works in April 1963 and allocated to Cardiff Canton (then 88A), it would be withdrawn in October 1975 from Plymouth Laira. *R. C. Riley*

Left: Down parcels train 3C07 has just left the parcels platform at Paddington station and is passing Subway Junction at the beginning of its journey west to Plymouth. The picture was taken on 19 October 1963, at which time No D7020 had been in traffic for just 20 months, having been delivered from Beyer Peacock in February 1962. Allocated from new to Bristol Bath Road (82A), the locomotive was to remain based at that depot until withdrawal in

January 1972 after a working life of less than 10 years. This class of 1,700hp Type 3s numbered 101 machines, four of which survive today in preservation, but No D7020 would be scrapped at Swindon Works in September 1972. *R. C. Riley*

Above: Proving that non-matching, multi-coloured rolling stock is not unique to the modern-day railway scene, an express for Wolverhampton Low Level via Birmingham Snow Hill sets off from Paddington on 19 October 1963 behind 'Western' diesel-hydraulic No D1049 *Western Monarch*. Seen passing Subway Junction, the train will travel via the traditional Great Western route to the West Midlands via Reading, Oxford and Warwick, as opposed to the ex-LMS line via Rugby and Coventry. Turned out by Crewe Works in December 1962, the locomotive would be withdrawn in April 1976, a victim of BR policy to standardise on electric transmission for its main-line diesels. *R. C. Riley*

Kensington Olympia was for many years the 'interface' between the Southern and London Midland regions and was the point at which cross-country trains changed locomotives. On Saturday 22 August 1959, having arrived behind 1,160hp BR/Sulzer Type 2s Nos D5009 and D5003, the 12.13pm Ramsgate–Derby Friargate will depart behind 'Black Five' No 45260, seen on the adjoining road. The diesels would later be transferred to Scotland, working freight trains before being withdrawn in 1975 from Haymarket (Edinburgh) and Eastfield (Glasgow) respectively as Nos 24 009 and 24 003. Kensington Olympia still sees direct trains between, for example, Manchester and Brighton, but today these are formed throughout by Virgin 'Voyager' multiple-units. *R. C. Riley*

Kensington Olympia had a mix of Great Western and BR semaphore signals, examples of both being in evidence in this picture taken on 6 October 1971. Passing light-engine is English Electric Type 3 (Class 37) No 6961, its 'D' prefix having been removed following the end of main-line steam in August 1968. Turned out by Vulcan Foundry in January 1965, it would assume its TOPS identity of 37 261 in 1973 and be transferred in 1982 to Scotland, where, named *Caithness* (from June 1985), it was to spend the next 15 years, many of them working on the Far North and Highland lines. Following withdrawal and sale by EWS it was to pass through various owners (including a brief return to Scotland in 2006 with West Coast Railways) and now works for Direct Rail Services, a subsidiary of British Nuclear Fuels Ltd. *R. C. Riley*

A magpie in Kensington? Having arrived light-engine from the locomotive shed at Old Oak Common, 'Warship' No D829 *Magpie* prepares to depart for the West Country with a train of empty six-wheel milk tanks from the sidings at Kensington Olympia on 4 October 1971, at which time the transport of milk in bulk tanks to London from the West Country was a significant traffic flow. The locomotive was to remain in traffic for less than a year after this photograph was taken, being withdrawn from Newton Abbot in August 1972. *R. C. Riley*

BR/Sulzer Type 2 No 5215 creeps through Kensington Olympia with a northbound parcels train on 6 October 1971. The first vehicle, although in blue-and-grey livery, appears to be of LMS origin and would thus be well into its fourth decade. Completed at Derby in July 1963 as No D5215, the locomotive would be renumbered 25 065 in March 1974 and withdrawn from Haymarket depot in Edinburgh in early 1981. Kensington Olympia has had a bit of a 'Cinderella' existence as a London terminus; after some years with a very limited passenger service it has in more recent times seen services direct to Manchester, Rugby, Watford and Brighton. Sadly its use as a major passenger terminus again seems to be on the wane, the Rugby service already gone and new franchise plans for 2007 and beyond suggesting the Manchester–Brighton cross-country service may also be withdrawn, leaving this large well-placed station with ample car parking very much a local station once again. *R. C. Riley*

Left: Photographed on 18 June 1986, Class 33 No 33 042 runs into Victoria station with the empty coaching stock of the Venice Simplon Orient Express Pullman train, which later that day would depart behind an electro-diesel on a lunchtime excursion to Leeds Castle in Kent, passengers alighting at the wayside station of Hollingbourne to complete their journey by coach. New in 1961 as No D6560, the Class 33 would have spent its career to date on a mix of passenger, parcels and freight traffic all over the Southern Region and was to remain in traffic for a further 10 years, ultimately being withdrawn from Stewarts Lane depot in October 1996. *Author*

Above: The presence of the GPO trolleys confirming that the train is a parcels service, Class 73 electro-diesel No E6027 stands on the west side of the old Waterloo station on 15 October 1970. Capable of drawing electricity from the

SR's third rail but qualifying for inclusion in this book by virtue of its auxiliary diesel engine, useful on non-electrified sidings and when the 'juice' was off, it was one of 49 such locomotives built by BR at Eastleigh in 1962 (the first six) and by English Electric's Vulcan Foundry at Newton-le-Willows in 1965/6. Among the latter, having been completed in April 1966, No E6027 would be the first to be withdrawn, in July 1972, following an accident. However, at the time of writing (March 2007) the vast majority remain extant, some in preservation, others still active on the national network. Although much of the famous Southern Railway terminus at Waterloo has remained untouched since this photograph was taken, the west side was transformed in the early 1990s by the construction of the new International station, built to handle Eurostar services to Paris or Brussels via the Channel Tunnel. *Author*

Left: Swiftsure meeting *Resolution* at Waterloo suggests a confusion between battles but in fact describes this encounter between two Class 50s outside the London terminus in June 1983. Both trains are Exeter services, which these locomotives worked so successfully between 1980 and May 1992, when they gave way to Class 47s (which in turn gave way to the multiple-units of today). Nos 50 047 and 50 018 had begun work in the North West in 1968 (as Nos D447 and D418 respectively) before being transferred to the Western Region and ultimately Southern Region duties. *Author*

Right: With the famous old white signalbox (left) standing guard over Waterloo station, Class 50 No 50 047 *Swiftsure* leaves Waterloo with the 17.20 service to Exeter via Salisbury on 18 June 1983. Built by English Electric at Vulcan Foundry in 1968 and new (as No D447) to the London Midland Region at Crewe in November of that year, the locomotive had been transferred to the Western Region in May 1974 and would be condemned in 1988 at Laira depot in Plymouth. *Author*

Above: July 1967 was a sad time for many enthusiasts, witnessing the end of main-line steam in the capital with the demise of this form of traction on the old LSWR line to/from Waterloo. Many photographers gave up in disgust, but thankfully on 8 July, just before the end, Dick Riley was active with his camera at Vauxhall, just outside Waterloo, where he photographed the up 'Bournemouth Belle' passing through the station. The most prestigious service on the Bournemouth line, this duty had been turned over to diesel traction some months before the end of steam. Six Brush Type 4s were sent to the Southern Region to help out, among them No D1922, completed by Brush at Loughborough in January 1966 and allocated to Cardiff Canton depot. Renumbered 47 245 in 1973, the locomotive was thereafter to lead an uneventful life, for many years being based at Tinsley depot in Sheffield for hauling freight trains. That was until 2006, when it reappeared on the national network in a pleasing maroon livery as the latest addition to the West Coast Railways fleet. *R. C. Riley*

Above right: From Waterloo the one-time LSWR main line to the West winds through South London but after Clapham Junction straightens out,

allowing expresses to get into their stride just four miles into their journey. Proving the point is this photograph, taken on 9 August 1975, of Class 33/0 No 33 003 racing through Esher station, 14 miles from Waterloo, with the 1V17 17.00 service to Exeter St Davids. Turned out by BRCW as No D6503 and placed in traffic from Hither Green depot (73C) in March 1960, the locomotive assumed its TOPS identity in February 1974 and would be withdrawn from service in June 1987. *Author*

Right: The double luggage vans giving an immediate clue as to its destination, a boat train from Waterloo speeds through Weybridge station in Surrey on Saturday 9 August 1975 *en route* to Southampton Docks, where it will connect with an ocean liner, probably a Cunard ship. The locomotive is electro-diesel No 74 004, at this stage of the journey drawing power from the electrified third rail. Built at Doncaster in 1958 as electric locomotive No E5000, the first of a class of 24 (but soon renumbered E5024), it had been fitted with an auxiliary diesel engine at Crewe in March 1966, emerging as No E6104. Having assumed its TOPS identity in 1973, it would be withdrawn in December 1977. *Author*

71

Left: Friday 30 May 1958 finds DEMU No 1017 leaving Cannon Street with the 5.14pm service to the seaside town of Hastings, just over 60 miles away. At that stage the space above the platforms here was open, many such termini having been built thus to allow the smoke from steam locomotives to escape. However, over the past 30 years or so Cannon Street, in common with a number of other London termini, has been reconstructed with office accommodation above the platforms. The 'Hastings' DEMUs were to remain in service until electrification of the line, this involving singling of the sections through tunnels, following which standard-width EMUs could be used. *R. C. Riley*

Above: BRCW Type 3 No D6509 basks in the afternoon sunshine at Hither Green depot on 10 June 1961. Built at Smethwick between 1959 and 1962, these 1,550hp Sulzer-engined locomotives weighed 77 tons. The backbone of the Southern Region diesel fleet for more than 30 years, they did a great job, whether singly or in pairs, on passenger, parcels or freight trains and in later years could be seen increasingly on the Western and London Midland regions. An unofficial yardstick of the success of a particular class is the number preserved or still in traffic; in the case of the Class 33s, of a total build of 98 locomotives there are 30 survivors, of which a handful remain active on the national network. *R. C. Riley*

Above: Situated near Lewisham, Hither Green shed (code 73C) has for years been an important locomotive depot in South London. Essentially concerned with freight workings, it was a subshed of Stewarts Lane (73A) and still sees modern diesels stabled on the site. When this picture was taken on 2 May 1959 the motive power was more varied, with steam and diesel types present in large numbers and with several different classes in evidence, 'Ns', 'Cs' and a 'Q1' representing steam and what would become Classes 08 and 24 representing diesel. Prominent are a number of recently delivered BR/Sulzer Type 2s, including Nos D5003 and D5005 — all kept well apart from the steam locomotives, which presented a significant fire risk. *R. C. Riley*

Right: Diesel-electric multiple-unit No 1032 races through Elmstead Woods station, between Grove Park and Chislehurst, on a Charing Cross–Hastings service in June 1960. These six-car units were built to Hastings-line gauge (*i.e.* narrower than normal stock) to cope with the narrow tunnels on the line between Tonbridge and Hastings. A number of 'Hastings' units survive in preservation and continue to be based at the St Leonards depot, near Hastings. *Derek Cross*

In steam days 'foreign' steam locomotives on Summer Saturday holiday excursions to the South Coast resorts had been a fairly common sight, but the advent of diesel traction rather coincided with a drop in demand for this type of railway journey. However, Dick Riley photographed one such working on 13 May 1976 deep in Southern Region third-rail territory. Formed of three Western Region Class 117 DMUs the 08.35 Oxford–Margate is seen passing Shortlands, with 64 miles to go before reaching the Kent coast. Such a journey in these suburban units can have been neither comfortable nor particularly quiet! *R. C. Riley*

Superpower on the Southern Region as 3,300hp 'Deltic' No 55 007 *Pinza*, more than twice as powerful as the regular SR diesels, powers through Shortlands station, between Bromley South and Beckenham Junction, with the 'Man of Kent' excursion from London to the South Coast. The photograph was taken on 15 March 1978, just over three years before *Pinza*'s withdrawal from service on the Eastern Region, its final depot of allocation being York. *R. C. Riley*

Almost-new BR/Sulzer Type 2 No D5007 approaches St Mary Cray Junction, south of Chislehurst and east of Bickley on the Chatham line, on 26 May 1959. Despite being only 12 miles from Central London this was a wonderfully rural location where in the late 'Fifties and early 'Sixties both Derek Cross and Dick Riley recorded a huge number of images of steam, diesel and early electric traction. The train is a down freight, destined in all likelihood for the Channel ports. No D5007 had been built by BR at Derby earlier in the year and although first allocated to Crewe South shed (5B) soon found itself on loan to the Southern Region. *R. C. Riley*

Taken seconds after the previous picture, this photograph shows No D5007 heading away towards St Mary Cray signalbox, partially hidden behind a tree on the right-hand side. The train is passing evidence of track-laying, confirmed by the presence in the foreground of the late-1950s four-wheel permanent-way vehicle; how track machinery has changed in the last 40 years. No D5007 would be renumbered 24 007 in April 1974, before being withdrawn from Eastfield in October 1975. *R. C. Riley*

Index of Locations

Full details of Ian Allan Publishing titles can be found on www.ianallanpublishing.com or by writing for a free copy of our latest catalogue to: Marketing Dept., Ian Allan Publishing, 4 Watling Drive, Hinckley LE10 3EY.

For an unrivalled range of aviation, military, transport and maritime publications, visit our secure on-line bookshop at www.ianallansuperstore.com

or visit the Ian Allan Bookshops in
Birmingham
47 Stephenson Street, B2 4DH;
Tel: 0121 643 2496;
e-mail: bcc@ianallanpublishing.co.uk
Cardiff
31 Royal Arcade, CF10 1AE;
Tel: 02920 390615;
e-mail: cardiff@ianallanpublishing.co.uk
London
45/46 Lower Marsh, Waterloo, SE1 7RG; Tel: 020 7401 2100;
e-mail: waterloo@ianallanpublishing.co.uk
Manchester
5 Piccadilly Station Approach, M1 2GH; Tel: 0161 237 9840;
e-mail: manchester@ianallanpublishing.co.uk